★ WHAT'S THEIR STORY? ★

Alexander the Great

D1513551

Oxford University Press, Great Clarendon Street, Oxford OX2 6DP

Oxford   New York
Athens   Auckland   Bangkok   Bogotá   Bombay
Buenos Aires   Calcutta   Cape Town   Dar es Salaam
Delhi   Florence   Hong Kong   Istanbul   Karachi
Kuala Lumpur   Madras   Madrid   Melbourne
Mexico City   Nairobi   Paris   Singapore
Taipei   Tokyo   Toronto

and associated companies in
Berlin   Ibadan

Oxford is a trade mark of Oxford University Press

Text © Andrew Langley 1997
Illustrations © Oxford University Press 1997

A CIP catalogue record for this book is available from the British Library

ISBN 0-19-910190-6 (hardback)
0-19-910196-5 (paperback)

1 3 5 7 9 10 8 6 4 2

Printed in Dubai by Oriental Press

Alexander the Great

THE GREATEST RULER OF THE ANCIENT WORLD

ANDREW LANGLEY

Illustrated by Alan Marks

OXFORD UNIVERSITY PRESS

Imagine ruling the whole world. That's what Alexander the Great set out to do, 2300 years ago. He led his army from Greece to India, and built the biggest empire ever seen.

Alexander was born in 356 BC in Macedonia, the most powerful state in Greece. His father, Philip, was the king. Philip had once been a handsome, dashing general, but now he was a battle-scarred old soldier, with a lame leg and only one eye.

Alexander's mother, Olympias, was tough as well. She had a fierce temper, and was quick to have her rivals and enemies put to death. She was very fond of poisonous snakes. It was said that she even kept snakes in her bed!

With parents like these, it is no surprise that Alexander grew up to be brave and adventurous.

MACEDONIA

Black Sea

ASIA MINOR

Mediterranean

Even at the age of twelve, Alexander showed how brave he was. One day he went with his father to see a fine new horse, a present from a friend. The horse seemed to be completely wild. It bucked and kicked and reared, so that no one could ride it. In disgust, Philip ordered it to be led away.

But Alexander saw that the poor animal was not bad-tempered. It was simply frightened – of its own shadow! The boy ran forward and turned the horse's head towards the sun. Now the shadow was out of sight, behind it.

Alexander stroked the horse until it was calm. Then he swung himself up onto its back and rode round the stable yard. Philip stared in amazement. Then, bursting with pride for his son, he gave him the horse to keep. It was named Bucephalus, and was to carry Alexander on all his greatest adventures.

The young Alexander was not just a fine horseman. He could run, wrestle, fight with a sword, play music and sing. Philip hired a famous scholar called Aristotle to be the boy's teacher. From Aristotle, Alexander learned about countries and peoples outside Greece.

Among the other pupils was a boy named Hephaestion. He quickly became Alexander's best friend. Their friendship was to last for the rest of their lives.

Alexander had his first taste of war when he was only sixteen. He was left in charge of Macedonia while his father was abroad, and he led an army against a band of rebels, and defeated them. But he had to learn about leadership very fast. In 336 BC, Philip was murdered – and Alexander became the new King of Macedonia. He was just twenty years old.

The news of Philip's death spread quickly. His enemies in Greece saw their chance to break free of Macedonian rule. Alexander had to show that he was as strong and ruthless as his father. The biggest threat came from the city of Thebes. Its people rose in revolt against Macedonia and called on others to join them.

At the head of his army, Alexander raced south and camped outside the walls of Thebes. He ordered the rebels to surrender. They refused. Alexander moved his troops to the city gates. Still, the Thebans would not give in.

Then came a moment of luck. One of Alexander's officers forced his way inside the walls and began fighting for his life. Alexander had to help him. His soldiers poured through the gates and smashed the Theban army. Alexander ordered the whole city to be pulled down. Only one house was spared – because a famous poet had once lived there!

MACEDONIA

Black Sea

ASIA MINOR

Cilician Gates

Issus

SYRIA

Mediterranean

Tyre

Siwah   Alexandria • EGYPT

Alexander was now in control of the Greek states. But this was not enough for him. He wanted to go on and conquer the vast Persian Empire to the east. Many years before, the Persians had invaded Greece. It was time to take revenge!

So the Macedonian army sailed to Asia Minor. The excited Alexander was the first man to leap ashore. He hurled a spear into the sand, to show that he claimed the land as his.

The enemy leader was Darius, the "Great King" of Persia. He had to be found and defeated. Swiftly, the Macedonians swept aside a strong Persian army. But Darius was not there. He had fled to Syria.

Alexander followed him. The quickest way to Syria was through a narrow mountain gap called the Cilician Gates, which was only as wide as four men. Alexander made a surprise attack at night. The Persian guards were so terrified that they ran away.

Alexander caught up with Darius near the town of Issus (in modern Turkey). His attack was swift and deadly. He captured the king's camp, but once again Darius ran away, leaving his soldiers to be killed by the invaders.

After this great victory, Alexander marched down the coast. He captured town after town, until he came to the port of Tyre. This was built on an island, and so its people thought they were safe from attack. They mocked Alexander when he sent offers of peace. They even threw his messengers over the city walls!

But Alexander was determined to capture Tyre. His men built a road out over the sea to the island. This took over half a year, for the sea was very deep. Giant catapults hurled stones to smash holes in the walls. Then wooden towers were pushed along the road. Alexander's soldiers poured out from them into the city. After a savage battle, the people of Tyre were forced to surrender.

Alexander moved on southwards to Egypt, the richest land on the Mediterranean coast. Here, there was no need to fight. The Egyptians welcomed him as their new pharaoh, or king. But Alexander had two important things to do.

First, he wanted to make sure of his power by founding a great new city. He sailed down the River Nile to the coast, where he ordered the city to be built. He even laid out its boundaries by taking flour from his soldiers' packs and sprinkling it on the ground. The city was called Alexandria.

The second journey was more mysterious. Alexander rode
far out into the baking desert, to the little town of Siwah.
Here was a shrine, where a great god called Amun could
foretell the future. Alexander asked Amun whether his
conquest of Persia would succeed. The god told him that
he would conquer the whole world!

Now it was time to finish the war with Darius. Alexander led his men deeper into Asia. At last they reached a plain near the village of Gaugamela, where they saw yet another Persian army.

It was enormous! There were more than 200,000 Persians. Some rode on war horses, some in chariots and some on elephants. The rest were foot soldiers. Alexander had only 47,000 men.

The battle began. At first, the Persian cavalry drove back the Macedonians. But then Alexander saw a gap in the centre of the enemy line, where Darius stood. Mounted on Bucephalus, he rode straight at the king. His horsemen galloped after him.

In his golden armour, Alexander was a terrifying sight. Darius, in panic, turned and fled. Many of his followers also ran away, pursued and hacked down by the Macedonian cavalry. It was a triumph for Alexander. He had smashed Darius's army and was ready to seize control of the giant Persian Empire.

There was no stopping Alexander now. One by one, the magnificent cities of the Persian Empire surrendered to him. The grandest of all was Persepolis, the capital city. In its vast royal palace, Alexander found an amazing store of treasure. This was soon loaded on to pack animals and carried away.

Then Alexander ordered the palace to be set on fire. Flames roared through the beautiful building, destroying everything but the stone walls. At first, the soldiers thought it was an accident, and ran to fetch water to throw on the flames. But Alexander stopped them. He wanted the palace to burn. It was a sign that he had defeated the Persian king.

Meanwhile, far away, Darius lay dead. He had been stabbed by his own generals. Now Alexander had no rival. He could call himself Great King of Persia.

A lexander now ruled a massive empire, stretching from Greece to Syria and Egypt. Surely this was big enough for him? But it wasn't. Alexander dreamed of being King of all Asia. He would go on with his conquests, until he reached the edge of the world! (In those days, of course, nobody knew how big Asia was.)

So he set off towards the east. And his soldiers followed. Alexander was such a powerful and inspiring leader that they would have gone with him anywhere.

They marched to Afghanistan and up into the mountains of the Hindu Kush. They trudged through ice and snow, gasping in the thin air. Their food ran out and they had to eat their horses and mules – raw. At last they came down on to the plains of India. It was here that Alexander married Roxana, an Indian princess.

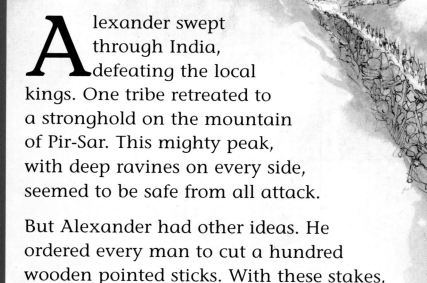

Alexander swept through India, defeating the local kings. One tribe retreated to a stronghold on the mountain of Pir-Sar. This mighty peak, with deep ravines on every side, seemed to be safe from all attack.

But Alexander had other ideas. He ordered every man to cut a hundred wooden pointed sticks. With these stakes, and tons of earth and rock, they began to fill in one of the ravines. It was over 200 metres deep, yet they built a bridge across in only three days.

At dawn, followed by 700 carefully
chosen soldiers, Alexander hauled
himself up the rock face and charged the
terrified Indians. Many were so desperate
that they threw themselves over the cliffs. In
a few minutes, the Macedonians had
captured the mountain.

Alexander had conquered northern India. And still he would not give up. His great warhorse Bucephalus died of old age, but Alexander marched on. In the end, his men stopped him. They refused to go any further. They were tired and scared and homesick.

Alexander was furious, but for the first time he was beaten. He agreed to turn back to Greece. He sent one half of his army by ship, led by his admiral Nearchus. He led the other half along the coast.

route taken by Alexander

route taken by Nearchus

Black Sea

MACEDONIA

Pella

ASIA MINOR

Sardis

Ephesus

Tarsus

Gaugamel

Mediterranean

Tyre

Bal

EGYPT   Memphis

He soon found that he was heading into a nightmare. He and his soldiers had to cross a desert of soft, scorching sand. There was no food, and little water. Anyone who fell ill was simply left behind to die.

Alexander suffered with his men. Once, a tiny trickle of water was found, just enough to fill a helmet. It was offered to Alexander. But he tipped it onto the sand because he knew his troops could not share it.

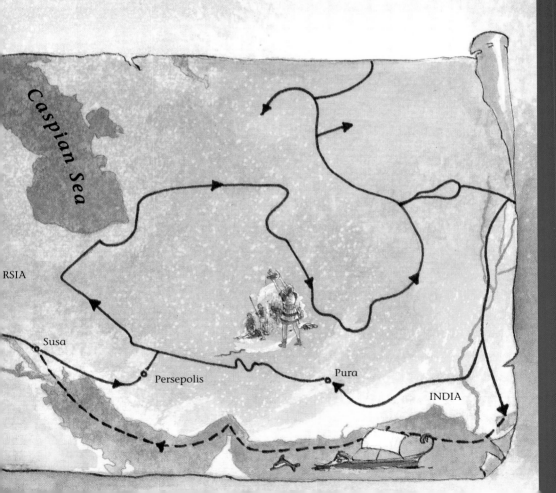

Caspian Sea

RSIA

Susa

Persepolis

Pura

INDIA

Alexander was not just a great general and a brave fighter. He wanted all the people in his huge empire to live together in peace. So he did not give all the important jobs to Greeks. Many Persians were appointed as governors.

When he got back to Persia, he invited ninety of his officers to a mass wedding. It took place in a huge tent, held up by pillars ten metres high, covered in jewels and hung with gold curtains.

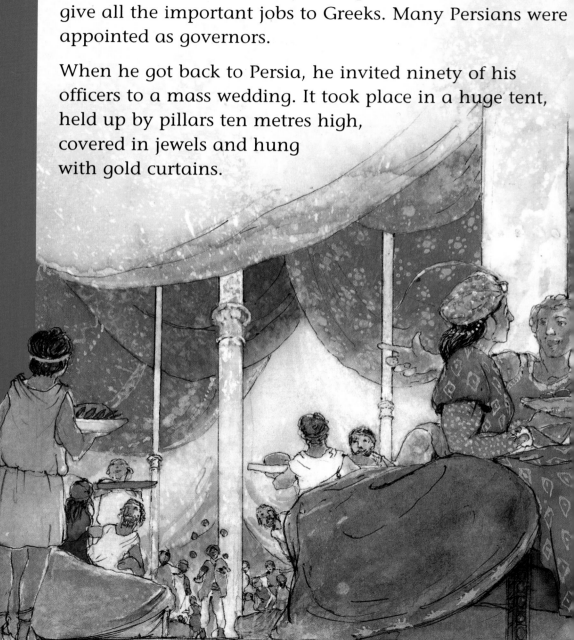

Here, the officers were married to Persian brides.
They had no choice – Alexander's orders had to be
obeyed! And besides, the emperor himself was marrying
a Persian princess as his second wife. This was his way of
uniting Greece and Persia.

As Alexander grew more powerful, his dreams became grander and wilder. He began to believe that he was a god. He ordered everyone to bow down before him. But at the same time, he grew sadder and more bad-tempered. When his dear friend Hephaestion died, Alexander wept for many days.

After a feast in 323 BC, Alexander fell ill. His many war wounds had left him weak, and his doctors knew that he was dying. His old army friends begged to see him one last time. As they filed past his bed, Alexander could no longer speak or move. Soon afterwards, he was dead.

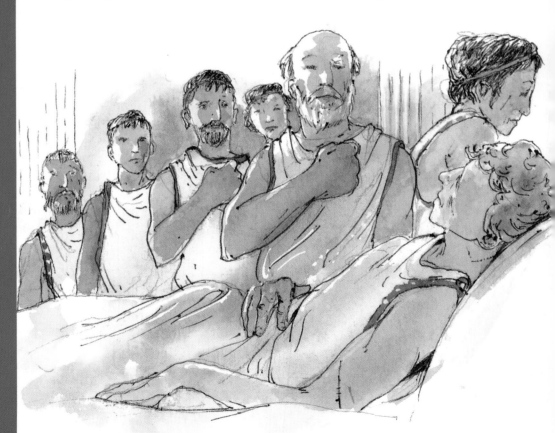

Alexander was just 32 years old when he died.
He is remembered as a heroic leader and the greatest
general in history. But he also changed the world.
By his conquests, he brought East and West together for
the very first time.

Important dates in Alexander the Great's life

356 BC Born in Macedonia.
336 Father is murdered and Alexander becomes king.
335 City of Thebes revolts: Alexander destroys it.
333 Begins conquest of Asia Minor. Defeats Persian King Darius at battle of Issus.
332 Reaches Egypt and founds city of Alexandria.
331 Defeats massive Persian army at Battle of Gaugamela.
330 Darius dies: Alexander becomes Great King of Persia.
330–28 Conquests in central Asia Marries Roxana, daughter of King Oxyartes.
327 Invades India.
326 Bucephalus dies: founds city of Bucephala. Army rebels and Alexander agrees to turn back.
324 Orders mass wedding of army officers to Persian wives. Hephaestion dies.
323 Dies, aged 32, after sudden illness. Buried in a golden coffin in Alexandria.

Index